Luminous Witness

Part One
The Poet And The Prophet
Poems by Stefan Visekruna

Part Two
Fall
Poems by Ljupka Palavestra

Two poets-a poetess and a poet-Ljupka and Stefan-come from the same corner of the world, same land, same tongue, linking their craft. They build bridges between the verse of their own voice and the foreign one they speak, just to share their messages. Though their poems hold different voices, Ljupka always searches for the light-even finds it in darkness-while Stefan plunges willingly into shadow, even though he is the poet of light. Her words touch you, heal you right away; his let you sit with the hurt a while, then quietly mend it. Two lights. Two cures. Two voices from one soil, one heart. Two soulmates.

Aleksandar Marić,
POETIKUM Publishers
Kraljevo, Serbia.

Collected Poems

© 2025 Stefan Visekruna and Ljupka Palavestra
All rights reserved.

Poems by Stefan Visekruna translated from Serbian into English by the Serbian-American poet Ljupka Palavestra.

Edited by Eleni Phufas-Jousma

No part of this book may be reproduced, stored, or transmitted in any form or by any means without prior written permission of the publisher, except for brief quotations in reviews.
Published by Ouranos Books, Inc.
www.ouranosbooks.org
[Ischua, New York, United States]

Index of Poems

Part One – THE POET AND THE PROPHET 1
   Poems by Stefan Visekruna 1
   When I Want to Kiss A Song 2
   Milica 3
   Trebinje 4
   They Don't Know About Bukowski 5
   Prisoners 6
   All My Thoughts Are… 7
   The Moment 7
   Fly, O Bird 8
   When A Woman You Have Loved Disappears 9
   Remarkable Insight 10
   The Sea 11
   Street Lights 12
   Hagia Sophia 13
   Can You See 13
   To Be 14
   Tears 14
   Carnation 15
   Captive Nightingale 16
   Love And Despair 17
   My Birds 17
   The Beggar 18
   When The Heart Falls Silent 19
   Wanderer 20
   I Don't Want The Past To Return 21
   I Carry A Bitter Song Within Me 22
   Longing Nights 23
   Poet And The Prophet 24

Part Two - FALL 27
    Poems by Ljupka Palavestra 27
    Oasis Of Peace 28
    Days Slip Away 30
    Tears Of The Rose 31
    War Storms 32
    Homeland 34
    Love Endures 35
    To The Man In This World 37
    Grandfather's Home 38
    Acceptance 40
    Merciful Souls 41
    Kiss 42
    Descendants 43
    Mothers Our Confessors 44
    Your Voice 45
    Don't Touch My Dreams 47
    My Mediterranean 48
    You Shimmer 50
    About The Forgotten 51
    Sun At Setting 53
    Ancient Fire 55
    Poems 56
    Still Stands 58
    Guiding Star 59
    Lies 60
    She Looked At The Sky 61
    Fall 62
Editor's Note 64
About The Poets 65

Part One

THE POET AND THE PROPHET
Poems by Stefan Visekruna

When I Want to Kiss A Song

When I want to kiss a song,
my soul quivers like a child in dawn,
eyes lifted toward the rising light—
Bright with wonder, flushed with delight—
Silent, yet trembling at a mystery
that pulls me into its secrecy.

Words scatter on the sea's warm breeze,
drifting upward with aching ease,
longing to climb the burning sun,
to touch the fire from which they've come.
I have dreamed of you endlessly,
chasing your steps through memory—
Caught by the radiance of your eyes,
lost in their tender, sweet surprise.

As the years drift on and on,
my love burns fierce, a glowing dawn;
for you are the summit in my chest,
The height my longing won't let rest.
A thirst for your lips consumes my breath—
A hunger deeper than life or death—
Such lips as mine have never known,
soft as a whisper, warm as a moan.

And this desire—bright and unconfined—
Lifts me to places undefined,
where shadows fall and senses rise,
and passion breathes beneath the skies.

Milica

You illuminated my suffering,
sheltered my melancholy,
kissing me
for a long, long time.

You appeared in my life
from a place
where no other woman came,
and that is an eternal joy,
a spring in my soul.

And your gentle and excited eyes
were shining in the night
like crystals, and were
looking, looking at me.

Darkness sneaks up deviously
upon me,
eroding my heart
with its rotten teeth
when you are not next to me.

My suffering is now noble,
and love is discovering you
softly as the drops of dew
on the grass.

We tremble and quiver with excitement
and we kiss even in the darkness
on the old road.

Trebinje

Bathed in sun and mellow wine,
my town of sighs lies half-divine;
my heart, my youth—both carried long—
Are hidden in a nameless song.
You shine with splendor, bright and free,
and offer all you are to me,
yet give yourself, with open grace,
to every soul in every place.
O trebinje—deep, enduring theme,
a romance greater than we dream;
beyond the centuries that span,
a love between the sun and man.

They Don't Know About Bukowski

They don't know Bukowski—
Who hasn't gone twenty-four hours without a drink
and then retched, dead drunk, in a tavern at six in the morning.

They don't know Bukowski—
Who has never tasted utter desperation.

They don't know Bukowski—
Who has never stared down suicide
and still taken one more impossible step forward
Into the hopelessness of the next day.

They don't know Bukowski—
Who has never felt, even once,
like the only human awake at dawn.

They don't know Bukowski—
Who wasn't first called mad by everyone,
and then revered by the same mouths.

They don't know Bukowski—
Who has never wagered their entire life
on the dangerous gamble of creation.

Bukowski was Bukowski—
Star-struck and gutter-born,
feeding and being fed upon by the fame
that circled him like wolves in Hollywood.

They don't know Bukowski—
Who has not waged war with themselves
at the cost of everything else that might have been called a life.

Prisoners

Prisoners do not feel the rain
that today pours bleakly down,
beating its relentless fists
against the old concrete that confines them.

Defiantly somber,
they walk through the rain,
granting it no significance,
and drift in quiet thought
across the boundless
horizons of imagination—
Their distant world
where they still envision a sunny day.

For it is not the worst of fates
to be hemmed in by walls,
bars, or barbed wire.
The worst is to be shackled in spirit,
buried in the ashes of one's own existence,
breathing each day the rancid,
damp air of isolation.

All My Thoughts Are...

I cannot look at you enough.
I have cried, and laughed,
and tapped my way through darkness,
listening,
searching for you
wistfully in the faces of other women.

All my thoughts are cheerful birds
rising toward you.

And I—like some intoxicated,
poor orphaned soul—
Can only gaze in wonder
at your beauty.

The Moment

When our eyes kissed,
my heart trembled in sorrow.
Forgotten wounds shot through me,
as I watched her leave.

Fly, O Bird

Carry away from the graveyard
those sluggish, illusory
dawns of a squandered life—
the verses burned,
the thoughts blood-bright.

Rest your wings, your weary eyes,
which all these years
have searched in vain
for embraces long lost to time.

When A Woman You Have Loved Disappears

When a woman you have loved disappears,
eyes turn aside from you
as if you were a stranger.
Bitterness rises through the chambers of the mind;
gray clouds descend upon the heart
like starving beasts.
The sun weeps into its own darkness,
birds fall mute,
water recoils from earth,
and smiles curl into the mockery of scavengers.

When a woman you have loved disappears,
you drift through books with sluggish fingers,
you stare into the morning fog,
you listen—hollow, suspended—
To the moonlight sonata.

Remarkable Insight

Before I knew you, my lord,
I believed this world to be the finest,
the ideal—better than any world that could be.
But when I came to recognize you,
I understood at last what beauty is:
true, eternal, unshadowed.

And from that moment,
the whole splendid world
collapsed before my eyes
like a tower of sand.

Since then, every vision of creation,
when set beside you,
has seemed only earthly,
only mundane.

The Sea

I come to you with fervor—
Humanity's eternal longing.
Chase away the clouds of turmoil
and receive me with your vast, unblinking gaze.
Release the muted silence caught
between your scorching, sharpened rocks
and the shattering of your waves,
and let it rise to meet me.

Street Lights

When darkness becomes a refuge,
street lights burn with the cold authority of the sun.
He wandered like a ghost in crisis,
muttering to the half-lit streets
while inhaling the damp rot
of stinking basements.

Dawn crept in, greedily devouring
what remained of the night.
The light burst in a dazed, indifferent glare,
and a stiff cheerfulness
briefly danced across his haunted face
before dissolving into the monotony of the day.

His eyes were red and raw,
sweat sliding down the corpse-like mask
he called a face,
and I watched him
with a disquiet I dared not show.

Then, in a hoarse, breaking whisper,
he said,
"Do you know the fastest way
to lose your sanity?
The fastest way
is dreaming of limousines
with no money in your pocket."

A ruined intellectual,
hollowed out by heroin,
stared at the hole in the wall,
dying, crying, yearning
for the sun.

Hagia Sophia

Hagia Sophia is an irremediable,
raw wound in the body of christianity—
A sacred grief that for centuries
has carried its dark destiny.

With a humbled heart
it lifts its gaze to christ,
awaiting the day
when healing will descend.

Can You See

Can you see how the light
pours its joy in trembling flight,
mesmerizing even the smallest things—
Insects, dust, the air it brings?

Can you see how life now stirs,
boils and dances as it blurs,
drunk with shadows at the edge of night,
swaying where the dark meets light?

Can you see how my own drunkenness
with dawns grows soft and limitless,
turning slowly, dream by dream,
into fantasy's quiet gleam?

To Be

To be severe with oneself—
Not in torment,
but as one drives a blade of light
through darkness.

Great is the anguish of the martyr who sings,
and, dying,
carves a poem
larger than life itself.

Tears

Tears fall—warm emissaries—
Fading along a pilgrim face
carved by struggles hidden beneath
this brief and fragile cloak of flesh.
Born from the hush of ruin,
They rise as quiet prayers;
and only heaven knows
where they wander, drift, or fly—
Burdened spirits seeking love.
They descend into the chambers
of time's hollow, ancient shell,
yet even as they vanish,
they reach toward the unseen light—
Toward the blazing, eternal sun
that calls all sorrow home.

Carnation

Pressed against the pavement,
a red carnation lies—trampled, forgotten—
Its petals darkened by rain and mud,
trembling in the early spring
like a small, starving prayer.

And then a thought rises—
Not in the mind, but in the heart's ungoverned depths—
That some wandering soul, aching through the world,
must look just like this:
a being wounded and luminous,
loving, suffering,

and quietly begging for forgiveness.

Captive Nightingale

As bandit clouds overtook the open skies and fierce rains scoured the earth,
so too did the captive nightingale weep.
Once his song had dazzled the newborn light of the universe,
but now it broke from him
as the cry of a prisoner whose soul has been shackled in darkness.

His muse dissolved into memory;
his home—once the whole unbounded world—was lost.
gripped by icy fears, he nearly forgot
that he had ever been free.
He felt himself a slave, condemned long ago
to row a galley for some ancient, forgotten crime—
A blind wanderer through endless night,
his trembling cane tracing the faint outline
of a freedom that had vanished.

Yet deep within a desolate, long-neglected ember of his heart,
a spark still lived—untouched, uncorrupted,
burning with the old fire of liberty.
And in that frail, persistent glow,
he became once more the nightingale he had been:
fierce with freedom,
and radiant with unquenchable love.

Love And Despair

Despair—that cursed wretch—has shrouded every path before us.
Her whisper is a venom that ravages the heart.
When i reach for you, when i long to touch or kiss you,
it is despair that closes over my eyes and darkens the world.

Fires and lightning flare through the depths,
lifting a wild song upon their mighty sighs.
I know too well: the love of a born wanderer
is a bitter torment—
A sky of mournful, crumpled thoughts,
all wounded by verses
and the long, restless road.

My Birds

My birds, tender and dear,
your songs never tire, never fade.
With each soft note you lift the dawn's pale veil,
opening the sleepy skies where dreams remain.
All my murmurs and longings you gather near—
You are my peace, my solace, my clarity,
a shield against the world's relentless play,
its small, sharp dramas that gnaw and fray.

Forgive me—
I have wandered, lost within my own maze,
caught in human folly and its heavy haze.
A shadow of sorrow presses on my soul,
yet your wings rise beneath me,
and make me whole.

The Beggar

Magnificent beauty overwhelms my sight—
The beauty of a youthful woman
who loves,
whose joy outshines the world's long night.
All dreaming has folded itself to sleep,
hiding deep
within a single, trembling song—
A song of love and sorrow's wine,
where tears and crimson longing twine.

How fiercely I yearn to rest
upon your lips—
I, the poorest beggar of love's vast quest,
a love that never slips
into decay, a love that cannot die.

So I will fashion only verses
For the nightingale's wandering cry;
and one day I will summon a poem
so burning, bold, and bright
it will melt the frozen giants
of Antarctica's endless night.

When The Heart Falls Silent

When the heart falls silent,
restlessness creeps in like a cruel mockery,
coiling despair within your gaze.

When the heart falls silent,
words tumble into cursed abysses—
Weeping, bound in chains of darkness.

When the heart falls silent,
barbaric onslaughts ravage your inner land without mercy,
and the dreadful penalty of loving
at last descends.

When the heart falls silent,
the sky becomes unreachable to man—
A vault of light sealed against him.

But when the heart falls silent,
you must gather all your strength
and rise above the ashes
of sin and death.

Wanderer

I was a street wanderer,
dragging a bruised love through the dark—
a half-drunk fool with a crooked smile,
chasing some distant scrap of bliss
I didn't have the guts to believe in.

I hunted sorrow in rain puddles,
bowing to the cobblestones
like they were gods who owed me nothing.
My soul stumbled, half-asleep,
soaked in tears,
and more tears.
Christ, how far the sun felt then—
Yet my trampled heart
kept beating in its corner,
refusing to quit.
I was a street wanderer,
still hiding that same sad love in the dark—
Still that passionate drunk with a twisted grin,
still dreaming of a little light
somewhere past the end of the block.

I Don't Want The Past To Return

You asked me why the sun feels distant now,
why its light no longer reaches us
with the golden certainty it once held.
Yet here we stand—aching, smiling—
Kissing the newborn day
as though we had been praying to love
for centuries,
kindling a holy fire in our chests
even while our wandering, mischievous eyes
traded secret winks with the darkness.

All my longing has risen into song,
and song has become a river of spirit—
Flowing, unbroken,
carrying fragments of our hearts
toward some unseen shore.
So I do not wish the past to return—
Not even youth's first trembling miracle:
that rapture of untested fire,
when the heart fluttered like a winged creature
and whispered its little prayers
directly into the ear of the sun.

I Carry A Bitter Song Within Me

The hardest part is facing
that my birds were nothing to you—
Their hymns, their bright wings,
their trembling dawn-fire
lost on a heart that never stirred.

Had even a single ember of their fervor
found refuge in you,
the storms would have broken around us,
the winds would have bent in awe.
We could have defied the world.

But now—
You stand as nothing more
than my ruined notre dame,
blackened and hollow,
smoldering in a paris
that died the moment you turned away.

Longing Nights

Soaked through—
Spring rain sliding down a wet face,
dripping into the hollow of longing nights.
Verses smolder in my chest,
burning like wine.

You gave me everything,
and I would give it all back
for a single song.

I love the storms in your eyes,
aching for heights beyond themselves.
I steal your love in the instant
the sea breaks open in your gaze.

The poet loves you—
Calls for you—
Even as every part of me aches.
And red wine spills my spirit out,
rising in clouds of tavern smoke.

Poet And The Prophet

The poet—the creator, the inspired one—
Bears a divine gift,
akin to the prophets of old.
Through life-giving words
he awakens and warns,
he teaches and lifts the fallen
from the mire of disgrace and death—
For his people,
and for all humanity.

Look into the ancient days:
the prophets were, in great measure, poets.
Poetry and prophecy walk the same path,
sharing one flame, one burden,
one mission of truth.

They meet in vision and insight,

in the love of justice,
in the fierce devotion to a kingdom
not of this world.
they meet in moments of revelation—
Epiphanic, theophanic—
Where the human heart
touches the breath of god.
The poet is appointed and chosen,
sent from above
to battle tirelessly
the wars of this world
and to bear witness,
with life and with word,
to the heavenly Jerusalem.

For poet and prophet are one tree,
rooted in mystery,
bearing the fruits
of sacred poetry
and blessed love.

And poets—
They are the incarnate,
ever-living conscience
of humanity.

Part Two

FALL

Poems by Ljupka Palavestra

Oasis Of Peace

I long to become an oasis
of peace and hidden love
for the one who suffers.
To be the hush in their day,
the quiet radiance
that pours itself into their sorrow—
To let them step
into the halo of my gaze
and find the stillness
their soul remembers.

Let them lay my hand
upon the wound that awakens,
let our tears intertwine
like pale rivers of moonlight,
joining as one
to follow the secret path
that leads toward the all-knowing.

And when storm-sadness
rises in my own eye,
when restlessness
tears the chambers of the spirit,
let me fold, weightless,
into my soulmate's arms;

let him gather
the fragments of this heart
until it glows again.

For hands—
Locked and laced
like sacred branches—
Open the hidden gates of heaven,
revealing the far-lit stars,
the ancient gift of light
ascending eternity.

Days Slip Away

Days slip away,
yet you remain inside me—
Untouched by time.
your eyes still gleam in the dark,
in that endless stretch
where memory breathes.

Nights roll on;
I burn alone,
cupping this small fire
in the hollow of my soul.
Days slip away,
but you are gone
from the room of this night.

Layer by layer,
tears glaze the words we shared
pearls from a cracked shell
still ticking with the pulse
of what once lived.

Days slip away.
What use is our love
in this blunt and waking real?
It lifts us—dreaming—
Beyond the hurt.

Days slip away;
I arrived too late,
our crossing folded shut.
Only ash rests in my palms,
only a restless cry
remains.

Tears Of The Rose

A scar on the heart,
a rose in the hand,
a tear in the eye—
For it has been cast
into storm-stirred land.

Its crimson petals bleed
as the rain drifts down,
soaking and stilling
its life grown thin,
its brief red crown.

Where do the sorrows
of such a flower fade?
Who dares to gather
the tears of the rose,
and tally what grief has made?

War Storms

War storms rose like creatures,
stealing the ground
from under our feet.
They herded us between cold walls
where the air itself
seemed made of screams.
We drifted through corridors
of broken hours.
We fell.
we rose—again, again—
Our wounds reopening
like doors that refused to stay shut.
We searched for the home we'd lost
in a world where crickets
forgot their voices,
where dusk arrived
without a song to its name.
We watched, through trembling tears,
as our home dissolved into dust,

and children grew upward
from the soil of pain—
Tall, solemn flowers
of a ruined season.
Sanity slipped—
For a moment stretched thin
across eternity—
A crutch that cracked
beneath our touch
the instant we leaned on it.
But not the soul.
She lingered.
She bled.
She breathed.
She gathered whatever light remained.
She loved—
Waiting for that distant,
uncharted day
when love ascends
to its forgotten throne.

Homeland

Sky gathered in a drop of dusk,
boundless stars fizzing wild,
and towering peaks
guarding the heart's old world.

Breathless, I cradled that beauty—
Love sparking endless,
rooted deep
in your lavish stone.
One child once danced with stars
across your night,
trembling even as playtime froze,
as years slipped past,
as breath grew thin.

Returning now is only
a midnight wish—
a slipping back
toward that humble cottage
set upon your quiet doorstep.

Love Endures

When every vision fades,
when holy stone houses
echo the wind's howl
through weeds and grass,
when the road home
climbs sharp with thorns—
Then the hearth-fire rises.

Voices of the dear ones gone…
I still see them
as gleaming stars
in sleepless nights,
keeping watch
over our wandering souls.

Mist has settled over
the houses of our childhood—
Joyful, flowered,
sweetened once
by wild blackberries.
Yet that warmth endures,
lifting us,
granting wings.

Roots cannot be torn out—
Not by exile,
nor distance,
nor curses spoken in anger.
The soul keeps its warm wing,
keeps candles burning
for centuries
in the sun-crowned church
of our birth-town.

Life's fury may tear the body,
but love—hunted, ragged—
still burns.

She lives
as long as breath
remains in us.

To The Man In This World

You are someone's sun,
someone's guiding star.
Someone breathes for your smile—
Do not dim it.
Guard the holy spark
burning inside you.

Someone draws breath
from your warm words,
finds belief again.
A life in innocent bloom
watches you;
a mother watches, too.
Yield not to darkness.

You are the mirror
of a clearer world,
unclouded.
You are the word—
But true.
Your tenderness
bathes another's heart.
Someone grows,
builds dreams,
and dares hope
because of your love.
Do not surrender.
Weather the black storms,
find meaning in tears,
wisdom in pain.
Rise from them all,
and walk on

Grandfather's Home

I dream of gentle hills
held in a hush so deep
it feels like the world remembering.
Dusk settles like velvet
over houses that seem to float,
and in that tender dimness
my soul keeps vigil in the mountains,
breathing the old flower-scent,
dreaming the same dreams
it once whispered to the stars.

I dream of harmony
bright butterflies
with sky-blue wings,
the quiet glow of lantern light,
the warm sparks
leaping from the fireplace.
And from the soul
a thin strand of sun rises—
Memory—
Sacred and fragile,
shivering like a candle
guarded by cupped hands.

I close my eyes in darkness
and the stone steps return,
leading me back
to the faces I loved.
I see eyes that shine,
smell the towering pine,
feel the wool blanket's weight
and the dawn spilling through the window,
Stirring something old—
Something once mine—
Back into warmth.

I am in that house again,
on the fragrant clearing
where my eyes first opened
to the sky—
and every part of me aches
to remain there.

Acceptance

Someone is truly magical
when they love—
When they embrace your flaws
and somehow make you better,
when they offer a brilliant smile
with eyes bright as the sun.

Someone is magical
when they listen,
when they understand
not just the words
but the ache beneath them,
when they chase away
your heavy fears,
when their voice warms you—
Hands far from yours
yet cradling you with ease.

That is when someone
becomes magical indeed…

Merciful Souls

Merciful souls
glimmer like rare gems,
their kind words
honey-sweet to the spirit.
They warm,
they radiate—
Divine dust
from distant stars.
a gentle hand from them
comforts,
guides you
from shadow into light.
But harsh words
fall cold and proud,
leaving the heart
unanswered.
And so we choose
what we become—
We grow our own voice,
for today,
and for eternity.

Kiss

You came in a dream—
The most tender,
most cherished presence,
your breath soft as an angel's,
your love carrying
the cedar-sweet scent of mercy.
Did you, in that instant,
lift a prayer toward me?
A bright breeze moved with you
as your lips brushed my neck,
and a pure, holy warmth
flooded my chest.
The ancient dream of love
was fading at the edges…
Yet it lived again
in that single kiss—
That sweet, small moment
that gave me hope
and lit the whole day.

Descendants

Descendants of wanderers,
they search for the lost again,
seeking the ancient walls of time,
the house of joy and pain.
Where once a candle glowed with peace,
a home the heart could claim,
they trace the warmth that used to be
and whisper the old name.
Tears softly touch the sacred icon,
set on a ruined nest,
so prayer may rise and shine once more,
and guide each child to rest.
So those who lead the young may carve
the memory pure and bright,
that holy ways endure in them,
that they may know their light.
They honor graves with tears of love,
the fallen held inside;
they lay a flower that never wilts—
A bloom that will not die.

Mothers Our Confessors

In you burns
a saint's unfading glow—
A tear born of eternity,
shimmering still
for me.
Into your arms I drift,
carrying the trembling whisper
of my soul.
Mother, though your form
dims in this world,
your presence moves within me—
Woven from the sun's
soft, eternal blaze.
And when the waves
bear us gently
into realms beyond sight,
our spirits will thread together
like star-fire,
bound forever
By love's unbroken strand.
Grieve not, beloved mother—
Be radiant,
be blessed,
fashioned from the first light
that ever touched creation.
And when a tear descends,
know that my love
shines holy,
unchanging.
And when I, too,
cross into the quiet beyond,
you will still live in me—
woven from the sun's
soft, eternal blaze.

Your Voice

Your voice—
Let it thunder into the vastness,
boundless as the breath of God,
weaving a radiant path
for wandering minds.
Let it lift the broken
on the stream of life,
soothe every hidden sorrow,
and offer Christ's
burning salvation.
In the exalted hills
your calling found you.
Nightingales stirred your spirit awake;
their songs braided themselves
into your very blood.
And in the sacred cloister,
while the world was still young around you,
you walked the corridors of silence,
seeking the fierce purity
of virtuous grace.
I behold your blazing
vision of God—
Sunbeams hunted
down rain-kissed paths,
your heart pursuing them
like a prophetic bird
building nests for dawn,
guiding the lost
toward the holy threshold
of new life.
Stand firm in the storm's roar—
Gentle, yet fierce with truth.
Let love be your sword of redemption,
your everlasting psalm.
And beneath God's mighty shelter,
Let your love endure the fire;
And when the burden grows heavy,

rise again—
Rise higher—
And soar.

(Dedicated to Stefan Visekruna, Serbian poet)

Don't Touch My Dreams

Don't touch my dreams.
They are the last bright country
where I can breathe—
A world still unspoiled
by your doubt,
your noise,
your shadows.
Don't bruise what is sacred.

Don't dim the fire in my gaze,
the wild, stubborn spark
that refuses to stop dreaming,
imagining,
loving out loud.
If you cannot see
the oasis burning in my chest,
then be silent—
Better your silence
than your cold hand
crushing what keeps me alive.

Don't trample the unseen flowers
that bloom inside me—
They are fragile,
yes,
but fierce with peace.
Even when pain wrings me dry,
even when my eyes lose light,
They guard themselves
in the deepest place.
So hear me—
Don't touch
what is sacred.

My Mediterranean

My mediterranean—
You are so far away now.
On icy nights,
I close my eyes,
and there you rise within me again.
I am reborn
from your azure depths,
bathed in the sun's
sparkling embers,
floating over your chiseled hills,
beneath your fragrant pines,
in reverie.
Seeking peace,
seeking shade,
I feel your radiance
mirrored in my pupils—
A glow that threads itself
through the very weave
of my soul.
I dream of your blossoming apricots
in the churchyard gardens,
your sweet mulberries
falling beneath their trees,
blue vineyards,
rosy cherries,
and the diligent hands

that plant and gather them.
And in this rainy, distant city,
I summon you—
Hold you in my trembling palms,
and press you close
to my heart.

You Shimmer

You shimmer—
Spilling grace
upon my heart,
a cascade of radiant sparks,
celestial joy
guiding me
with a noble soul
and loving me
with all-seeing eyes.
You hide a tender longing
in your breast,
yet you sing it
in the melody of your spirit,
scattering fragrant
rose petals of desire.
Born anew,
like the rising sun,
you blaze—
Ablaze with
luminous splendor,
wondrous being
of light.

About The Forgotten

I will write of those
no one writes about—
Of those for whom
no one cares.
of the lost,
the sick,
caught in a web
of fear
and terror.

I dreamed a dream
and saw their eyes—
gleaming,
dark,
and hollow;
silent despair
within them,
and yet
a fierce dignity
still alive.
They beg
for someone
to give them a voice.
Their suffering
has lasted too long
behind hospital walls—
Too long the screams
no one hears,
too long the shame
that clings to them,
though they
are not to blame.

A soul
slipping toward hell,
a psyche
losing ground
and balance,
a hand
that loses hold
of the hand
of salvation.
A heart
that pleads in sorrow,
weeps,
and seeks forgiveness.
Do not steal.

The fragile peace
they struggle to find
with insults
or mockery.
God sees
their sorrow.

(Dedicated to people who struggle with their mental health.)

Sun At Setting

My sun at setting,
bathed in radiant hue,
you slip away gently,
your whisper fades through—
A tender murmur
melting my heart anew.
It speaks… I love you too.
Your warmth drifts deep
into my dreams,
where in my soul you breathe
with quiet gleams,
a light that wakes
what darkness ever seems.
I see your path—
The narrow, faithful line
you walked through thorns
that could not dim your shine;
you left the scent of roses

pure, divine,
a grace the heavens
once called wholly mine.
The sun slips down
to join the waiting sky,
to rise in realms
where blessed visions lie—
to dawn in dreams
no earthly night can deny,
and crown the kingdom
where eternal mornings fly.

(Dedicated to my mother Zora)

Ancient Fire

Where everything is ablaze and alive,
where grass flashes gold in the sun,
where the cherry tree pours out
its red-sweet dream—
The river runs sky-blue and green,
swift, clear, undone.
Where cracked hills cradle
their stone-built homes,
and bread tastes honest,
warm as honey's song.
Where the blue thorned flower
in the scrub still blooms,
fierce and alive,
though the days grow long.
Herzegovina—
Sun-bathed, wine-bathed—
You endure in the heart's
deep choir.
Even when roads loop wild
and wander away,
even when rivers sweep us
beyond return,
your call burns higher.
Paradise of the soul,
faith-draped,
heroes crowned in earth and air—
Sacred ground,
where ancient fire
forever blazes,
and your shining stays eternal,
bright and rare.

Poems

Poems born of ice-cold loneliness
and grief,
polished by bright tears—
Their roots sunk deep
in sacred ground,
their angel-wings brushing upward,
reaching for eternity.
Rhymes the heart strings behind it,
rhymes that drift forever,
rhymes that bind the dim field
to the wide sky—
Rhymes that call back tenderness,
that guard love
from dying.

Songs that long
to crown mercy,
to rescue beauty
from forgetting.
Songs reborn at dawn,
forging meaning
out of cries,
begging sunlight.
Songs—
This holy melody
that cleaves to the past,
releases tears,
and colors the moment
alive.

Songs—
The threads to God,
spun from worn earth,
from sacred earth.
They come
like newborn children,
breathing mercy—
These golden threads
of the soul.

Poems,
poems,
poems.

Still Stands

Still stands—
The defiant wall of our house,
gone gray,
split,
yet unbowed,
tireless
and faintly gleaming.

Wars and years
have carved their furrows deep,
yet it stands,
admonishing.
In the city of green rivers—
Rivers that carry days,
carry years,
back into the currents
of childhood—
Still it stands,
whispering:
our inheritance is holy.

My first breath
stirred within her warming stone—
And still she stands,
grieving our distance.
Roots guard us;
love ripens its vow;
sorrow endures
yet remains cherished—
A chosen bond
for eternity.

Guiding Star

You would have been my rescue,
my guiding star—
the sweetest breath upon my lips,
the dew that gathers
when the heart can't speak.

You would have been the flower-trail
that leads the soul to God,
your mind so noble,
steeped in wisdom's nectar,
depths of knowing
I longed to fall into
and never rise from.
Swallows would have carried
your trembling yearnings—
Those fragile, fluttering wishes—
on their translucent wings
toward me.

You would have been
the firm stone of strength,
the wide river of solace,
the wings of hope.

I reached for in the dark…
But you remain only longing,
a silhouette of what might have been,
the ache behind my ribs—
and you,
you are not here.

Lies

Lies strike like beasts—
They bite, rip,
and feast on the soul,
leaving it raw,
bleeding,
echoing with cries
no one hears.

Lies—
Black, venom-soaked—
Stab with the crooked blade
of betrayal,
twisting deeper
each time trust tries to breathe.
They scorch everything they touch,
branding the heart
with their poison,
searing truth
until it curls like ash.

Lies do not wound by accident—
They hunt.
They stalk faith,
suffocate hope,
and claw at the sacred light
inside a person.
They come to reign,
to rot,
to ruin—
To tear down whatever stands,
and laugh
as goodness falls.

She Looked At The Sky

She looked longingly at the sky,
searching for a sign,
searching for God.
So much pain weighed on that heart—
So many lonely nights
had carved their furrows
into her weary face.

Someone cruel
had betrayed her,
broken her heart,
wrung every tear from her eyes.

She prayed—
Spoke to God of her wounds,
begged him to place
a little hope
inside the next dawn.
But still
the shadow followed her.
She lifted her gaze again—
And saw lilac clouds,
sunlit and trembling,
caressing her heart
with sudden beauty.

She reached toward God,
called out to the dear souls
who loved her—
And slowly
she began to smile,
to rise.
Wiser now,
more joyful,
and nearer to him
than ever before.

Fall

This fall
blooms like spring,
when love's tender smile

surges through
the chambers of the heart.
Twilight weaves itself
into a celestial radiance
that stirs my waking—
And resurrects
my soul.

Editor's Note

This book was shaped across distance—two poets separated by an ocean, yet closely connected through experience, memory, and an uncommon attentiveness to language. My work as editor involved careful reading, light revision for clarity, and many thoughtful exchanges about order, tone, and image. What struck me early on was how little intervention the poems themselves required. Again and again, the task was not to improve the work, but to reveal it more clearly by listening: reading closely, clarifying where needed, and discovering that very little needed to be changed in order for even more their beauty to emerge.

As I moved through these poems—often returning to them after time had passed—I was reminded of how rare it is to encounter writing that deepens rather than diminishes upon rereading. The poems gathered here carry emotional precision, restraint, and a quiet seriousness that does not ask for attention but earns it. Editing, in this case, felt less like correction and more like listening. A particular pleasure of this collaboration was the conversation around visual elements: original drawings and photographs that do not illustrate the poems so much as accompany them—echoing their atmosphere, pauses, and silences. Selecting and placing these images became an extension of the same attentive process, guided by respect for the poems' inner space.

Publishing is my most recent vocation, following four decades spent teaching college writing and, earlier still, navigating questions of language and expression in a household shaped by immigration. That long attentiveness to words, to what is carried and what survives translation, guided my work here. Perhaps for this reason, I am especially drawn to work that speaks quietly, carries memory with care, and trusts the reader. These poems do exactly that, and it has been a privilege to accompany them into print. This book embodies those qualities and the qualities that the values of Ouranos Books seeks to present to the public. It has been an honor to bring these poems together in a single volume and to shepherd them into print.

About The Poets

Stefan Visekruna is a Serbian poet, born on December 9th, 1991, in Trebinje, Bosnia and Herzegovina. He studied theology in Belgrade and has published five books of poetry and short stories in the Serbian language.

Ljupka Palavestra is a Serbian American poet born in Mostar, Bosnia and Herzegovina in 1977. She has a bachelor's degree in art and a master's degree in mental health counseling. She worked as an advocate for people with mental illness. She has two books of poetry published in the Serbian language. Ljupka worked on the translation of Stefan Visekruna's poetry for this book as well as did some of the illustrations. She lives and works in Buffalo, New York.

List Of Illustrations

Original Artwork by Ljupka Palavestra
Original Photography by Stefan Visekruna

Fly O Bird (Photograph) 8
The Sea (Artwork) 11
When The Heart Falls Silent (Artwork) 19
Wanderer (Photograph) 20
Poet and the Prophet (Photograph) 24
Oasis Of Peace (Photograph) 28
Grandfather's Home (Artwork) 38
My Mediterranean (Artwork) 48
Sun At Setting (Artwork) 53

www.ingramcontent.com/pod-product-compliance
Lightning Source LLC
Chambersburg PA
CBHW041403090426
42743CB00006B/143